Lion(ness)

Awakening the Warrior Spirit Within

Dr. H J Muhammad

Dr. H J Muhammad

Printed in the United States of America
First Printing 2021
First Edition 2021

10 9 8 7 6 5 4 3 2 1

Photo Credit: Lion Portrait, by Johan Swarepoel,
photographer, Adobe Stock

Lion(ness)

Table of Contents

Prologue...1

Chapter 1 5

The Introduction 5

Chapter 2...11

From A Cat To A Lion...*11*

Characteristics of a Lion...11

Three Lions 14

Lion in Biblical Context 16

Chapter 3...19

The Problem..*19*

Step 1: Learning the Knowledge of the Devil 19

Who is the Devil? 21

Chapter 4...27

Bow To The Creator Or Bow To The Created?...................*27*

Step 2: Learning the Knowledge of God 27

MGT & GCC Vanguard..31

Misconception of Women in Islam 42

Predator and the Prey 43

Chapter 5...49

Fuck Or Fight *49*

Step 3: Assessing the situation 51

Step 4: Calling on Allah (God or the Creator) and

releasing your inner lion...51

Poetic Combat..54

Alpha Male vs. Beta Male 60

We Fight with Those who Fight with Us 62

Step 5: Retreat and Seek Refuge in Allah (God) 66

Walking in my own atmosphere 71

Chapter 6 77

Healing From Battle 77

Chapter 7 89

The Five Steps To Awakening The Lion (Ness) Spirit Within

In Review 89

Chapter 8 95

The Lioness As A Leader 95

A Special Thank You 105

Prologue

I was inspired to write this book because of a great need. This book was written as an attempt to answer the question that has been posed to me by so many people who are anxious to understand how I became such a mentally and spiritually strong individual. I will share some of my life experiences that have contributed to my "lioness" spirit.

If you are reading this book, it is because your spirit has led you to this body of work, and it should be used as an instrument to help you find the lion(ness) or spiritual warrior within. Too many people have not yet found the lion(ness) within and are comfortable playing the role of domesticated cats. There is a time to be meek and humble, to be in a place where one is nurtured, admired and protected. However, this role offers limited growth and development, and the domesticated cat can become a keepsake with little expected change.

For many, living as a cat is acceptable. For others, there is a desire to transform into the lion that can roam this society freely without reproach. This is not a book for those who fear the lion(ness) within; it was written for the cat that desires the skillset to transition into a lion. To survive and prosper in this society, to move outside of the domesticated cat's prescribed lines and limits, one must become a lion.

A lion is a predator, a fierce protector, and a leader. As a predator, the lion is seldom, if ever, prey. I have learned to identify the roles of predators and prey in our society, and I hate the predator-like behavior that has been perpetrated on God's people by wretched and savage individuals. In my fifty years on this earth, I have been the victim of—and have witnessed—the barbaric actions of human predators on human prey, and it sickens me. I have seen people accept the role of prey, not knowing that there is a choice; that they can be a predator, that they can be a lion. The choice is theirs.

The roles of predator and prey are apparent in work environments, business relationships, and societal interactions. They are even apparent when one simply walks down the street. There is knowledge in learning what role one plays in any given situation. Once the domesticated cat leaves the house, it must learn how to be a predator. Without the safety of the house, the cat is, indeed, prey. Humans constantly behave as either predator or prey; that is the nature of the societal jungle in which we exist.

This book explains how we can identify the roles, and it provides lessons on how we can change roles from prey to predator. Merriam-Webster defines a predator as an organism that obtains food by killing and consuming other organisms, and one who injures or exploits others for personal gain or profit. Prey is defined as an animal that is hunted and killed by another for food. Those are the roles.

Transforming into a lion's spirt is not a simple task. Society demands that they be prey, so many people settle into that role. I have been blessed to have spiritual guides, physical instructors, and the grace of Allah to assist me with my growth into the lion's spirit. People see and feel the lion's spirit within me. I am often asked how I can easily transition from a cat to a lion in seconds. To answer, I would share some of my life experiences, but I never felt as if I gave a complete answer. This book gives the complete answer.

There are five steps to awakening the warrior spirit within: 1) Learning the knowledge of the Devil, 2) learning the knowledge of God, 3) assessing the situation, 4) calling on Allah and releasing the inner lion, and 5) retreat and seek refuge in Allah (God). Now that you are reading this book, you will tap into my spirit, the very spirit that led you *here*. Here, where I will open up my heart and soul to you. Here, where I will share my successes and failures in hopes that my story will inspire you to incorporate the Five Steps to Awakening the Warrior Spirit Within.

Chapter 1
The Introduction

I entered this world prematurely on March 22, 1970 from the loins of a Puerto-Rican man and the womb of an Ethiopian mother. Yes, this sister got *culture*, but I didn't grow up being taught the practices or beliefs of either culture. However, I was taught two principles as a child: "Do unto others as you would like them to do unto you," and "Fight with those who fight with you!"

As my life was beginning, my oldest sister's life was ending. Rhonda died at the age of 2 of Sickle Cell Anemia. I entered this world as a replacement gift to my mother as she was losing her firstborn. My sister's death created a sadness that I have carried my entire life. She was taken from me before I could even get to know her. I still fight with myself to come to grips with her death and to accept it wholeheartedly without survivor's remorse.

Education is treated like an option in many Black families, but not mine. I come from multiple generations of military personnel, and in our family, it is mandatory to either go to the military or college. Functioning without a plan is considered foolish and unacceptable.

I chose college. Why? Because "Big Donna" went to college. Big Donna is my beautiful, funny, and independent big cousin. She is affectionately called Big Donna because we have a little Donna in the family who is named after her. Her name helped us identify the eldest Donna from the youngest Donna in the family. Big Donna is the very cousin I worshipped, and she was the first to choose college over the military. She was everything I wanted to be.

People blossom at different stages of life. In high school, I did better than a lot of my teachers thought I would, but I didn't blossom. College, however, is where I fell in love with learning. It was right around the time I was introduced to the teachings of the Most Honorable Elijah Muhammad and was awakened spiritually, emotionally, and intellectually. A feminine god was born, and it translated into my studies.

I attended Columbia College Chicago for undergrad not because I wanted to, but because my parents would not let me go away to college. My dad said he had the final word on where his money would go, which would be a college in Chicago. Columbia College it was.

While at Columbia, I studied the teachings of the Most Honorable Elijah Muhammad, Black world leaders, metaphysics, psychology, humanities, ethics, all eastern religions, and world culture. I was like a sponge absorbing knowledge like it was a liquid.

I credit a conversation with my late dear sister and close friend Dr. Steffie Turner (May Allah be pleased with her) with my graduate education. I shared with her my desire to be a lawyer as a young girl. I informed her that while I still desired to protect and fight on the behalf of others, I no longer wanted to pursue law. I had become disappointed in the judicial system, and my disappointment led to me changing my subject matter for school.

Steffie recommended Industrial/Organizational Psychology as a way to fuel my desire because it entails fighting for others inside of organizations. After that conversation, I researched several schools and chose a school that was well respected in Chicago. I chose to enroll at Roosevelt University to pursue my master's degree. I knew once an employer saw that I had graduated from Roosevelt University, they would want to retain my great talents and move to promote me within the organization.

I thought I knew how to study, but the volume of work on top of working in corporate America and forming my own tribe with my new husband and two daughters was taxing. I was no longer in my early 20s. I was now in my early 30s and had been out of school for almost 10 years. However, my graduate goal was achievable with a loving and supportive husband who was willing to pick up where I slacked in cooking, cleaning and caring for our children. He understood that this was a sacrifice I was making for our family. It was quite difficult, but my mom and husband pushed me when times were tough. I greatly appreciate their emotional and physical support.

My graduate experience proved to be a learning experience that re-shaped my thinking. My graduate education inspired me to be more analytical in my thinking, and analytical thinking was needed for me to be a lion(ness). My ability to analyze situations has led me to successfully read a situation for what it is and to respond appropriately.

Education helped me develop a strong academic discipline that contributed to my lion(ness) spirit. Self-discipline is necessary to awaken the lion(ness) within. It helped me to be forbearing and to be able to endure difficulty. A lion(ness) must be strong like a lion and be able to endure to the end. My Master of Arts in Industrial/Organizational Psychology was earned with blood, sweat, and tears. I graduated knowing how to be a true leader. I thank Roosevelt University; their leadership preparation is immeasurable. Well done, Roosevelt!

Despite the trauma of graduate school, my love for education persisted. Once again, I allowed Steffie to encourage me to continue my education and obtain a doctorate, like she had obtained. She was such a blessing to me. She was the sister who helped me identify my strengths and how they benefited those around me. She was the type of friend who believed in you and helped you believe in yourself. She is surely missed, and her passing left me with a hole in my heart.

My doctorate from Argosy University is the jewel on my academic crown. My stretch from an above average high school student to earning an Ed.D. in Organizational Leadership from Argosy University, an M.A. in Industrial/Organizational Psychology from Roosevelt University, and a B.A. in Marketing Communications from Columbia College Chicago was academically fulfilling. Thanks to Steffie's encouragement, my degrees have helped me to become highly intellectual, and my education and leadership experience in the areas of banking, sales, management, consulting, customer service, education, law enforcement and security have qualified me to lead and to teach others.

Life experience and education have taught me that it takes a certain type of spirit to successfully navigate life. One that will stand strong to opposition and one that will be strong enough to endure to the end. In my 50 years on this Earth, I have learned that life requires a lion(ness) spirit to achieve goals, to have self-protection, and to achieve happiness. In this book, I introduce to you five steps that have helped me awaken the warrior spirit within: 1) learning the knowledge of the Devil, 2) learning the knowledge of God, 3) assessing the situation, 4) calling on Allah and releasing the inner lion, and 5) retreat and seek refuge in Allah (God).

Chapter 2
From A Cat To A Lion

In my early years, I was merely a pussy cat. I was a young woman with no spiritual identity. I was jumpy and fearful, always avoiding confrontation. I was only willing to fight or defend myself when my back was against the wall, literally or figuratively. Well, Allah had a whole different plan for me! He wanted to turn me into a lioness, and he did not consult with me. He just put me through trial after trial until I became a lioness and awakened the warrior spirit within.

What's this talk about lions?

Characteristics of a Lion

Let's talk a little bit about the characteristics of a lion. For thousands of years, lions have been considered to be one of the most feared and bravest animals in the animal kingdom. Lions are part of the feline family and have built quite a reputation for being a symbol of bravery and courage. They live in grassy plains, savannahs, open woodlands, and scrub country. These landscapes allow these hunters to creep through vegetation and leap upon their unsuspecting prey.

Lions are the only members of the feline family that live in large groups called "prides." Prides consist of about fifteen lions, mostly female lion relatives and their young. Lions within a pride are often affectionate and enjoy good fellowship with lots of touching, head rubbing, licking and purring, but the males are territorial and will roar and use scent markings to establish their domains.

There are distinct differences between the male and female lion. Unlike the lioness, the male lion is not sheltered. The male lion has it very hard because when he is first born, its every man for himself. Male adolescents are chased out of the pride by their fathers and become nomads. They will either link up with another nomad lion or be by themselves.

Once the lion grows up and learns to hunt, he will find a female or find a pride. If he finds a pride, he will kill the old lion, kill the cubs, and take over the pride. Males patrol their territory, protect the pride from intruders, and hunt large prey.

Lionesses learn from watching male lions. Lions are family oriented and roll in a pride with other lions because they know hyenas (natural enemy of the lions) are always lurking.

The male lion protects, but the woman hunts. The lionesses are nocturnal and work in teams to stalk and ambush their prey. They help male lions hunt large prey like zebras and wild beasts. They are strategic. The lions encircle a herd from different angles, and can run in short bursts up to forty miles per hour to catch prey, killing the prey by biting it on the neck.

The female lion is a hunter and the first teacher of the pride. She teaches the adolescents and children how to hunt, and will call the male lion only if she needs his assistance. She is the *Queen*, and he is the *King* of the pride. The babies eat first, then the men, and then the women eat.

I learned how to be a lioness by watching and listening to the wisdom of the men in my life, or shall I say the male lions in my pride. The head of my pride was my grandfather. He demonstrated how to lead. He was the educator, protector, and nourisher of the pride. He taught me the importance of trusting your instincts and maintaining loyalty to the family.

Three Lions

I have three uncles—or lions—who taught me valuable lessons. The first uncle, Uncle Joey, taught me martial arts and how to defend myself against male predators. He also introduced me to Caribbean culture and music, and that introduction led to my attraction to West Indian men, which is why I am married to one today, but that is another story!

Uncle Joey was always showing me karate moves to use whenever a man tried to attack me. God! It was like he knew the future, but little did I know that my mother told him to toughen me up due to my small premature stature. I didn't understand the power in those lessons when I was a little girl. I just thought they were cool. I loved spending time with Uncle Joey.

The second uncle, Uncle Willis, taught me how to make things happen. He always challenged my way of thinking when I complained about something. When I was a freshman in high school and was complaining about our local cable station not having Black Entertainment Television (BET) as a channel and how it was not fair, he challenged me to do something about it. I told him I didn't know what to do. He suggested starting a petition and having students sign it. I accepted the challenge. When I came back to him with the petition, he was impressed. I was so elated that I impressed him and also proud of my growth and development.

Uncle Willis took the petition to his job and had his co-workers sign the petition. I then took it to the local cable station, and a couple of months later I received a letter stating that BET would be added to the viewing selection. However, the company wanted me to know that my petition did not contribute to their decision because more than half of the signers did not live in our area.

I was confused and took the letter to my uncle. He explained to me that my petition was the reason BET was added, and that the company just did not want to credit a teenager with forcing change. He congratulated me and told me that "this is how you make change; complaining does not make change."

Although he is no longer among us, I cherish this lesson and many more that he's taught me, like learning how to drive, learning about cars, learning about music, and, most of all, learning not to let things conquer me.

The third uncle, Uncle Alonzo, is quite the man. He taught me how to spot a male predator at the age of 7. I learned how to recognize the games that men play on women—the street game. I would watch his actions. I remember him telling me to, "watch this!" He would run up to girls and say something to them, and then they would respond in a manner that he was hoping for like a smile or handing over their phone number. Each time, he would turn around and look at me.

Later he would say to me, "You see how easy it was to get her? I just told her what she wanted to hear!" Boy, was I educated, man! I now knew the game. He often told me that men would use my hazel eyes as a tool to try to get me on my back. He prepared me for this world and taught me that the prize is always the woman. I was educated and equipped to navigate successfully through the game of life. The game of conquering women!

Lion in Biblical Context

Why would Almighty God Allah place so much emphasis on the lion in scripture? Is it because he is fond of the animal that he created to be the "King of the Jungle?" If you said yes, you are incorrect. Allah placed so much emphasis on the lion in scripture because He wants us to focus on the spiritual characteristics of a lion.

In the book, *The Second Mile* by Sarah H. Terry, the lion is described as a symbol of strength and power, a symbol of great virtue. The lion is one willing to suffer, is strong in defense of what is right and wrong, and strong in protection. Let's also add courageous and fearless, not accepting defeat and unwilling to be conquered by other animals or elements in the jungle. A natural leader!

Now that we have evaluated the characteristics of a lion, let's transfer those characteristics to a real human being. Bear with me! This is not a new concept; it has been done before, but in scripture.

The lion is the most mentioned and most revered animal in the Bible. In the "Book of Revelation," Jesus the Messiah is referred to as a Lion. That is parallel to the Snake mentioned in Genesis and growing to a Serpent in the "Book of Revelation." "The Book of Revelation" is a duel between the snake and cub, who have grown to be the serpent and the lion (Genesis" 49:9-10).

Growth from a cat to a lion is a process. It is one that does not happen overnight. It didn't happen overnight for me, just as it didn't happen for Jesus as He grew from Jesus, the son of Mary and Joseph, to Jesus the Messiah.

Chapter 3
The Problem

There is a grave problem in American society. Many people are steered toward religion to learn the knowledge of God, but religion, as it is practiced in this society, is used as a tool to control the minds of the people. One who controls the circumference of your thinking controls your actions.

You must first learn the knowledge of the Devil before you can learn the knowledge of God. Who—or what—is the Devil? It is not some spooky character that lives underground in a fictional place called Hell!

Step 1: Learning the Knowledge of the Devil

The Devil starts within. The devil is the thought that causes you to act in a manner that is in total opposition to the will of Allah (God). How can I start a path to Allah

(God) without having the ability to identify, name, and conquer the devil from within?

Conquering the devil within is how you become god in flesh. Once I accepted the teachings of the Most Honorable Elijah Muhammad, I took an oath to submit to do the will of Allah, and to submit until I became a god in feminine form. Going from a devil to a god is not easy, nor is it a short journey.

I am an avid reader and love to soak up knowledge through reading. I read all of the books of the Most Honorable Elijah Muhammad. I read *Message to the Blackman, Our Savior has Arrived, Fall of America*, and *Eat to Live* Books 1 and 2. Each book helped me to gradually accept my own and to be myself. I was awakening.

Eat to Live Books 1and 2 introduced me to the "Eat to Live" diet, which requires you to eat one meal a day. Eating to live consists of eating healthy foods like meats, fruits, and vegetables. It results in you eating less food while allowing your body to digest the meal from the previous day. This gives your body time to eliminate the previous meal before ingesting your next meal. One meal a day is strongly recommended in the teachings of the Most Honorable Elijah Muhammad.

Once I mastered one meal a day, I graduated to eating one meal every other day. After mastering eating one meal every other day, I went to eating one meal every three days. You must master your diet in order to master your thoughts and your actions.

Who is the Devil?

"The only devil from which men must be redeemed is self, the lower self,

If man would find his devil he must look within: his name is self. If man

Would find his savior he must look within; and when the demon self has

Been dethroned the savior, Love, will be exulted to the throne of power."

—Noble Drew Ali

Early in my adulthood, I asked Allah to guide me and to give me his coloring, which means his perspective, his wisdom. I remember at the about the age of 17, my mother orchestrated a situation where she allowed my cousins and me to drink alcohol. The agreement was this was an experiment for learning purposes only, and not an endorsement to drink. A discussion would take place at some time after the event. I don't remember what I was allowed to drink, but I got drunk, of course. I was demonstrating so much love and was having fun.

Immediately, it turned bad. I tried to fight everyone in the house. My family informed me of my violent actions and how genetically I responded to alcohol. I responded to alcohol just like all my other relatives. Alcohol was the instrument that was used by individuals in my family to destroy family relationships.

I was also confronted with the future choice I would have to make: choosing to drink to be accepted by my friends, or choose to end the generational curse by deciding not to drink at all. I did not like how the devil in myself was unleashed by the consumption of alcohol. I chose to abstain in order to control the devil within and end the generational curse. The devil within was contained and controlled until the next test by Almighty God Allah.

I remember playing softball with a group of sisters from the mosque. A few taunted me while I was at the plate, teasing me about being from the West side of Chicago. All of these sisters were from the South side. You have to be from Chicago to understand the rivalry. It was like some sort of sibling rivalry that lingers on even to today. Westside vs. Southside and Southside vs. Westside. The rivalries are pointless, being that Black folks don't own or run their communities on the south or west side!

Their voices were like braising hyenas. This lion was angered! I was so angry that I threatened them all with a bat. My exact words were, "I bet you won't step to this plate talking that Westside shit!"

Now, they were over 20 feet away and no real threat to me. They were just teasing, but my ego deceived me into thinking they were serious. They were only being competitive, and they knew the teasing would rattle my ego. A lion or lioness must know when there is a real predatorial threat, and when there is not.

The devil within was wickedly wise by convincing my ego that there was a threat. The devil within grew to be wickedly wise and more cunning in deceiving the God in me. The God in me was not wise enough or trained enough to defeat the devil, and it took years before I would learn the wickedness of the devil within. The devil within is the voice inside your head that persuades you to act in rebellion to the word of God. The devil within mislead me into thinking that other women could not be trusted. My lack of trust resulted in me pushing away women who were of high character and would have contributed to my spiritual growth and development. I did not learn this until my late 30's and that was far too long. Now that I have learned to control my ego and open my heart to trust, I have successfully surrounded myself with spiritual women who continue to nurture me on a daily basis.

I will share with you a time in my life where I acted like a devil in my first marriage. I remember having a heated argument with my ex-husband about his infidelity. I was livid, beyond angry, and I walked away from him. I had no control over my anger at the age of 22.

Instead of allowing me to cool off, he wanted to force me to work it out with him. He grabbed me to force me to listen to him, and out of extreme anger, I pushed him into the wall so hard that he went straight through the drywall.

I immediately ran to the phone and called my grandparents' house to talk to my Uncle Joey to tell him that my ex-husband had hit me. Uncle Joey is a fighter, and I was determined to manipulate him by exaggerating the truth. I was going to lie to my uncle because I wanted him to come over to my apartment and beat up my ex-husband.

The devil plans, but Allah is the best of planners. The wrong uncle answered the phone. Uncle Willis answered the phone. This was not a part of my plan because he is not the fighter; he is the level-headed one, the analyzer, the peacemaker. Damn, my plan was thwarted! I asked him to pass the phone to Uncle Joey, but he heard the anger in my voice and asked me what was wrong. I angrily told him to put Uncle Joey on the phone. He refused and asked, "Why, so he can come over there and beat him up?"

Allah is so merciful. He thwarted my devious plan to destroy my ex-husband and manipulate my uncle. I was being a devil. What if Uncle Joey had answered the phone? He would have heard the distress in my voice and driven fifteen minutes to my apartment to possibly beat my ex-husband to death. My uncle could have earned an assault or attempted murder charge, and my ex-husband could have been seriously hurt or killed. I am so grateful that Allah was in control and His will was done. The devil within me was controlled, not by me, but by Allah!

In the teachings of the Most Honorable Elijah Muhammad, we are taught that everyone has a self-accusing spirit. The self-accusing spirit is the voice of the god within. Every time the devil wins, the voice of the self-accusing spirit gets quieter and quieter until you can no longer hear it. Every time you listen to the self-accusing spirit, the voice gets louder and louder.

Jesus the Son of Joseph and Mary conquered the devil within to become Jesus the Messiah. Jesus became the Messiah by learning who the Devil is first and learning who God is second. He conquered the devil within by submitting to the god within and listening to the voice of the self-accusing spirit. In the *Self-Improvement: The Basis for Community Development* study guides, in a speech dated Dec. 12, 1986, Minister Farrakhan, the national representative of the Most Honorable Elijah Muhammad, and my dear minister, expressed the importance of participation in self-examination, self-analysis, and self-correction in order to quicken the self-accusing spirit in all of us.

I remember Minister Farrakhan giving the Muslims in the Nation of Islam an instruction to attend Friday night study group every week. I obeyed the instruction, and I have grown to reap the benefits. It was through self-examination, self-analysis, and self-correction that I learned to master the devil within, which led me to fashion and develop the god within myself.

Chapter 4

Bow To The Creator Or Bow To The Created?

In your journey to know thyself, you will come to discover the god in you. The journey for the Devil and God starts from within.

Step 2: Learning the Knowledge of God

Once you learn the knowledge of the Devil and the knowledge of God, you will instinctively know when to recognize both in you. Now you will be faced with a decision: bow to the Creator, the true and living God, or bow to that which He created, which is man.

How does one choose bowing to man over bowing to God? Every time we choose to accept and practice that which is contrary to the laws of God, we are bowing to man. In society, evil is rebellion, but it is acceptable behavior. Men and women who actively hunt each other sexually for sport are praised and honored by the masses, but this behavior is shunned upon by God. This is an act of bowing to the ways of men and not bowing to God.

Choosing to restrain from high sexual activity with strangers is an example of bowing to God and living the prescribed life. It is against the laws of God to steal, and when we refrain from committing theft, we are bowing to God. However, those who steal objects, money, and the hearts of men are thieves and choose to bow to the created.

Bowing to Almighty God Allah, means you bow only to His thinking and His prescribed way of life. You bow only to truth. Embrace what is from Him (scripture, moral character, etc.) which is truth, and you reject what is not of him (practice of evil, deception, manipulation, destruction, death, etc.) which is falsehood. Representation of Allah will become imbedded in your character. It will become who you are and what you practice. You won't be the only one affected by your decision to bow to Allah, and His way. Bowing will ultimately affect those around you.

The only authority is truth and standing on truth without picking sides will result in you bowing only to the Creator. My wonderful mother Bobbie, as she is affectionately called by family, has been my biggest example of standing on truth regardless of who is affected by it. She bows only to the Creator.

I went into my second and current marriage without learning anything about marriage. My first marriage ended within two years because of my ex-husband's infidelity. In the third year of my second marriage, I had to learn maturity. My immaturity prohibited me from seeing truth. I was a young woman of 27, highly emotional, and very dramatic when things did not go the way I wanted them to go. I was a "jinn," a fiery spirit, as described by The Holy Quran.

> *"And surely we created man of sounding clay,*
>
> *Of black and fashioned mud fashioned into shape.*
>
> *And the jinn. We created before of intensely*
>
> *Hot fire."*
>
> *—Holy Quran 15:26-27*

I was blowing things out of proportion, starting arguments, demonstrating controlling behavior, and always looking for an out to end my marriage and destroy my family. My mother is a woman who stands on truth and refuses to take sides. She remains loyal to truth.

Ok, let me explain!

I remember early in my second marriage; I acted like a spoiled brat. I threatened to leave my husband after every argument and repeatedly stated to him (how should I put it?) "You ain't my Daddy." This is the attitude that many Black Women have today. The sad part about it is I was not raised like that, nor did I hear that from my mother or grandmother.

I called my mother one day after an argument with my husband and told her the girls and I were moving home with her and my Dad.

"No you not!" she replied angrily. "Let me ask you this, is he beating you?"

I said no.

She asked, "Is he cheating on you?"

I said no."

She responded with, "Grow up and stop comparing him to your father. Your father got him by over 20 years. What are his faults?"

I answered with about five things.

"Is that it?" she asked. "Well, let me run down a list of your dad's faults."

She listed about ten things and said, "I'm not done yet. What you need to do is stop looking at your dad through child's eyes. Your dad is not perfect. You, in my opinion, went out and found a younger version of your dad. Now, grow up and make your marriage work!"

Click!

I was in shock! I stared at the phone for about a minute. *I know she didn't just take his side.* Well, it was tough love and it was shock therapy. It was what I needed to grow up and respect my husband and my marriage. Truth. Don't you see how powerful it is? My momma stood on truth that day and still to this day!

MGT & GCC Vanguard

One of my coworkers told me I was the strongest woman he had ever met. Wow! I was not *one* of the strongest, but *the* strongest woman he'd ever met. Whether he was being truthful or not, his words were riveting! In that very moment, I thought, "I'm winning!" After feeling like I was losing for so long, I was actually winning!

He asked me how I became so strong. My answer to him was that I was not a phenomenon; I am one of many women who have chosen to stay obedient and faithful to Allah. The encounter with that brother humbled me and made me think of the powerful men and women who contributed to the development of the lioness within. He was one of many who have asked me how I came to be the lioness I am today. I must share my origin in the teachings of The Most Honorable Elijah Muhammad and the individuals who helped Allah fashion and shape me.

My faith, my complete trust in Allah, comes from the teachings of the Most Honorable Elijah Muhammad, as taught to me by Minister Louis Farrakhan. There are seven units that govern my life: how to keep house, how to rear my children, how to take care of my husband, how to sew, cook, and, in general, how to act at home and abroad. I believe that Allah came in the person of Master Fard Muhammad. My faith has been strongly impacted by my spiritual guide and teacher, Minister Louis Farrakhan.

I walk in this world knowing that I am not *of* it. I am here only to serve as a portal, a conduit, to serve as a communicator between the physical and the spiritual realm. Translation? I am here to be a servant of the true and living God, Allah. Allah is my source of energy and in my womb, in my soul, I found the true and living God in me in feminine form.

I am and always will be an MGT (Muslim Girl in Training) and GCC (General Civilization Class) Vanguard (young women from the ages 16-35). I remember attending Jumu'ah prayer at the Orthodox mosque. I noticed that all the Black Muslims were in the back of the mosque. I also noticed how the women were treated as less valued. I questioned a very close sister about my concerns. She called me Malaika. "Malaika, you are too Black and need to go over there with Farrakhan." I was so hurt by her response and could not understand why a Black Woman would be offended by that question. At that moment, I knew I did not belong there. I was destined to search for those who loved self just as much as I loved self.

Well, I would finally get my wish. I ran into an old classmate in my neighborhood. I remembered him because one of my good friends in school had a serious crush on him. It's been well over 25 years, but I think his name was Anthony.

I saw him at the bus stop. I stopped and offered him a ride. He recognized me and got in my car. I noticed he was wearing a kufi (a hat Muslim men wear). I asked him was he a Muslim and he nodded yes. I told him, "I am too." When I asked him what mosque he attended he answered with, "The Nation of Islam." I told him how much I wanted to go the mosque and he told me I could go with him on a Sunday. Two weeks later I picked him up and we drove to the mosque.

Upon arrival, he explained the search procedure and seating requirements to me. Everyone is searched for weapons upon entering, and men and women do not sit together. I was ok with that because I had already learned of the search procedure and seating arrangements from a friend.

Anthony dropped the bomb on me when he informed me that that Minister Farrakhan would not be speaking that day, and that Dr. Khalid Muhammad would be the keynote speaker. He was excited, but I frowned with disappointment. I wanted to leave at that point. He immediately assured me that Dr. Khalid Muhammad was a great minister and that I would not regret staying. However, if I still wanted to leave, he would understand. I trusted his opinion and decided to stay to hear this brother. We said our goodbyes and agreed to meet up after it was over.

When we approached the door, a pleasant brother with extremely smooth and clear skin greeted us with As Salaam Alaikum (Peace be unto you). He opened the door and I was instructed to go to the woman's search area while Anthony went in the search area for the men. I was greeted by the most beautiful sister I had ever seen.

"As Salaam Alaikum, Sister!" she greeted. "Welcome, to Mosque Maryam!"

I immediately felt unworthy to look that sister in her eyes. Her energy vibrated high, and she glowed like the sun. Every Muslim I passed glowed and was very friendly and kind. They made me feel at home. I said to myself, "Now, this is more like me. I love my people!"

The meeting opened in prayer, and charity was collected. A minister came out to bring on our featured speaker. Out came this short, dark-skinned, bald-headed, muscular brother wearing African garb and toting a sword. He looked like a Black Yule Brenner. Damn, I was in love! He spoke with fire and strength. Each word struck the audience like loud thunder in a rain shower. People were literally cringing and rocking back and forth in their seats.

He spoke on how Minister Farrakhan was not listed in the latest *Ebony* Issue as one of the 100 most influential Black men in America. He asked the audience to raise their hands if they or anyone in their household owned any issues of *Ebony* or *Jet* Magazines. Over 90 percent of the audience raised their hands. He made a bold promise to Johnson & Johnson Publishing Company that if Minister Farrakhan was not listed in the next issue as one of the most influential Black men in America, he was going to bring everyone that was at the lecture that day to their headquarters, located on South Michigan Avenue in Downtown Chicago, to drop all those old issues of their magazines and burn them in front of their building.

I was fired up! In my mind, I immediately started locating all my mother's old issues of *Ebony* and *Jet* magazines. I mentally prepared to gather them for the event. Needless to say, the event never happened because word got back to Johnson & Johnson Publishing, and they listed Minister Farrakhan in the next issue.

I had never heard a Black man talk with that much courage, boldness, power, and strength. He touched a part of my soul that had never been touched before, never been cultivated in that way before. He awakened the soldier in me; he awakened the lioness.

After the meeting, some younger sisters approached me. They told me they recognized the soldier in me, and that I was what the MGT/GCC Vanguard was looking for: a soldier between the ages of 16-35; a soldier willing to give her life for the education and protection of our people. They explained that they handle the security for the women in the Nation of Islam.

"We work with the FOI (Fruit of Islam), men in the Nation, to secure our Black Nation," a sister explained.

I was instructed to become a member, and after I became a registered member in the Nation, I became a Vanguard.

I was in love, but not in a sexual sense. I had fallen in love with the truth, the mission of resurrecting Black People, but most importantly, the sisterhood. I had met

God in feminine form. I came into the understanding that there was the place I become a god. I joined the Nation!

I came into the Nation at the age of 19 and under the guidance and leadership of the MGT Captain, Betsy Jean Farrakhan, respectfully called BJ. She was a captain over all the women in the Nation of Islam in the late 80s and early 90s.

BJ was a beautiful and tall Black Woman. She was very strong and also the oldest daughter of Minister Farrakhan. She was one of the strongest women I had ever met, and I was intimidated by her beauty, height, strength, and title. Most of all she was an older woman with confidence, and that was difficult for me to consume because I did not understand what that meant and how important it was for any woman and how important it would be for me in years to come.

She was so hard on me. I was assigned to her security detail, and she would designate me as the point, the lead security person in any movement. I would screw up so much, and she would yell at me. I shared my discontent with another sister on the security detail, and she assured me that BJ liked me and that it wasn't what I thought. She even suggested that I speak to the captain about my concern. The suggestion scared me to death, but I did it.

I pulled BJ to the side and asked her why she was putting so much pressure on me. I communicated to her that I didn't know what I was doing, and I had become very frustrated about the situation. She smiled at me and told me, "You are a soldier, and Allah does not put anything on you that you can't handle."

I became a changed woman after that encounter, elated that this grown woman, a woman of her stature, believed in me. Little old me! My confidence in my security abilities grew and I became a fierce security officer. I obtained a leadership position and trained women to proficient levels of security.

I grew in my security like I grew in my Islam. I was Vanguard in my studies like I was on that security. I was front and center at Friday study group like Minister Farrakhan ordered the believers to be, and I learned well. Little did I know that my obedience to being in study group would save my life spiritually, emotionally, and physically. Study of self is the study of God. The study of self is mastering the devil within in order to be god.

My studies developed a high level of self-love and security. Security on a higher level—not just security of a dignitary or principle, but security of the heart, the mind, and the soul. I submitted and I opened my heart and mind to Allah, and He came in and rewarded me by putting me in the presence of great teachers like Minister Wali (May Allah be pleased with him), Minister Ava Muhammad, and Mother Tynetta Muhammad (May Allah be pleased with her).

Minister Wali was patient with me, pulling me aside and coaching me on the truth. I gave wrong answers in study group. I was probably the youngest in the study group, wrong as too left shoes, but his spirit inspired me to study, and he would advise me on where to find the truth. I am so indebted to him. I love you and miss you, Big Brother.

Minister Ava Muhammad is true power of God in feminine form. I sat in her study group and she had to spank me a lot! She would often say, "Sister, where did you get that answer? I'm going to need you to study if you are going to be in my study group."

Study? Well, I came back on my Mustaqim, prescribed life for a righteous Muslim to live. I came back on my knowledge and was a powerful force to reckon with because I was a sword being shaped in the fire and the forging wasn't finished. Allah was still shaping me.

I was selected to secure Minister Ava Muhammad, giving me a close and personal look at a powerful helper to Minister Farrakhan. Not only was she a minister in Islam, she was a prosecuting lawyer. She came with a very impressive resume, and I had the honor to protect her as she represented the elevation of the Black Woman to the world. I learned how to conduct a lecture, how to defend the teachings of The Most Honorable Elijah Muhammad, how to carry and deliver power and truth in feminine power. You can't be that close to someone and not be touched by their spirit. I have no problem debating truth because she was my example. It was my pleasure to secure her and to keep her safe. Google this sister. She is on YouTube and has written several books.

What can I say about Minister Tynetta Muhammad? She cultivated my love for crystals. I remember securing her on a detail. I drove while my security partner rode shotgun. We assisted Minister Tynetta into the back seat. She got in the car with a small bag. She informed me that what was in the bag was fragile, and I should be mindful. When I asked what was in the bag, she pulled out a quartz crystal skull. It was spell-bounding. I asked her if it a female or male crystal. Her eyes sparkled as she said, "Oh sister, I don't know." In that moment we bonded over a love for crystals. Our entire ride was about crystals of different types.

Allah put me with someone who would sharpen my spiritual side. I was becoming a double-edged sword. My soldier side was sharpened well while serving my time securing Minister Ava. The spiritual side of my sword was being sharpened as I spent countless hours securing her while all the while soaking up her vast knowledge of the teachings of the Most Honorable Elijah Muhammad and the Holy Quran.

My high level of security earned me a spot on the elite Honor Guard team, the elite soldiers of the MGT. Becoming a member of this team was like being a Navy Seal in the United States Navy.

I continued to secure Minister Ava and Minister Mother Tynetta, but I also got the opportunity to secure Minister Farrakhan (we worked with the FOI when securing him), Mother Farrakhan, and Winnie Mandela. There were other celebrities as well, but there was no better honor than securing Mother Farrakhan, as she was and is the mother of our Nation. She is strong, beautiful, and powerful. She taught me balance. I was too strong, often too much for the men in Islam, but she taught me to balance that strength with femininity. Now, who can top that? Right, no one!

I was honored to secure Winnie Mandela in New York at the very first Holy Day of Atonement. I had just finished a long detail in NY and was tired due to a lack of sleep. I was laying down for a couple of hours when I was awakened by sharp knock on the hotel door. I was taken to a meeting where I and a few sisters were selected to secure Winnie Mandela. My dear sister Dr. Steffie Turner was one of the chosen sisters. I was in shock! Like I'm talking Winnie Mandela, the wife of Nelson Mandela, a South African anti-apartheid revolutionary!

There was a threat on her life, and my number was called. I answered with no fear. I was the point, the lead, and we handled business. The one thing I can remember about her was her humility, her ability to trust a group of young women in their early twenties with her life, and the life of her comrades who traveled with her. Priceless. Don't tell me Allah is not the true and living God! My soldier is eternal!

Misconception of Women in Islam

When the average person is asked to describe a woman in Islam, strength is not a word that comes to mind. However, once people get to know me or have witnessed my level of strength, they go into a state of shock when they find out I am a Muslim woman. There is a misconception that Islam abases the woman. That is far from the truth! Islam *liberates* the woman.

In the introduction of the Holy Quran it states that men and women are spiritually equal. There is no sexism in the TRUE teachings of Islam. If you witness Islam being practiced in a way that the woman is abused or mistreated, it is not TRUE Islam. Surah 58, titled, *The Pleading Woman*, is evidence of this truth.

In Surah 58, the woman is pleading with Allah about her mistreatment from her husband. Morally, men of this world are supposed to be our husbandmen. They are supposed to be our protectors, our providers, our nurturers. Not our tormentors. In my trust in Allah, I challenged him like the woman in Surah 58. In times of danger, sadness, and travail, I acted out the role of the pleading woman, and He answered me every time. In times where wicked men were trying to manipulate, control or destroy me, He answered my plea and empowered me when needed or surrounded me with angels when He desired protection in numbers to prove to the environment, to the world that when woman submits to Him, He will protect her at any cost.

Predator and the Prey

America has become a society of predators. Merriam-Webster defines a predator as an organism that obtains food by killing and consuming other organisms, and one who injures or exploits others for personal gain or profit. Merriam-Webster defines prey as an animal that is hunted and killed by another for food, one that is helpless or unable to resist attack: victim.

To be human prey is to accept the fact that someone or something else is God over you. I didn't like being lorded over and decided to stand up to the predators. In standing up to the predators, I discovered that they are not brave and courageous like a lion, but loud and deceptive like a hyena. The so-called predators want you to fear them because they fear you.

It is imperative that the lion understands who she (he) is in order to help the hyena understands who she (he) is. These hyenas are walking around with role ambiguity, not knowing their role. They perpetrate the life of a lion. Don't fret! As a lion(ness), you will take great pleasure in helping them realize who they are and not what they *think* they are in society. It is the duty of the lion as the ruler of the animal kingdom to control the animals of the kingdom. As the righteous, the ones with the spirit of a lion must maintain ethical, moral, and spiritual order and balance in the land. Ask yourself, are you a lion or a hyena? Lions don't need other lions to help them make decisions. Lions stand alone. Hyenas are dangerous animals that roam in packs preying on other animals or weak people.

Look at the violence perpetrated among women, the co-creator of God. In man's eyes, Woman is the problem, but in God's eyes, Woman is the solution. In the world of White Supremacy, women have no value. We are only here for men's sexual pleasure.

America practices a patriarchal society, a society where the woman has no value. This is in contrast to the African people, who practice a matriarchal society where women are valued and contribute to the governing of their nation. This concept is one of great importance because it sets the building blocks for the devilish behavior that is perpetrated against women everyday with no remorse.

We are living in a time where predators are preying on women like never before. Domestic violence, sex trafficking, and rape are rampant in America, especially among Black women. As women, we can't look at violence against women as isolated incidents. It is bigger than any one woman. Today some unknown woman, tomorrow you or me. An attack on one woman is an attack on all women. Are you ready? Are you ready to roar?

It is time for Woman to accept the fact she has been preyed upon by predators, dangerous predators who prey upon others like hyenas. These hyenas are weak and choose to empower themselves by preying on women. It is imperative for Woman to know who she is in order to protect herself from the predator. She must accept the fact that she is the co-creator of God, and humanity was birthed through her womb. Once realizes this, she will tap into the feminine power of God.

In my years of working in the prison system, I was faced with the likes of men who dedicated their time to the disrespect and ill treatment of women. The pinnacle of my role as a correctional officer in a predatorial environment came on January 7, 2019 at 7 a.m., in the seventh year of my employment with this organization. I went into the shift office to ask the shift clerk a question. The shift clerk for the day was a white male officer whom I rarely spoke to or barely knew. I asked my question professionally and respectfully, and he showed a disdain for my question, responding with great disrespect, sarcasm and lies.

I firmly instructed him to respect me as his elder and to respond to me with respect. He immediately slammed his pen onto the desk and told me he was sick of me (which was puzzling since I hadn't interacted with him). He stood up and rushed toward me, pushing past another male officer, and stood two feet from my face. I was in complete shock! I was facing a violent and angry man who appeared to be more than six feet tall, weighing well over 200 pounds.

My mother taught me that if I ever had to fight a man that I should pick up anything I could get my hands on to defend myself. I quickly scanned the area to find something to use in my defense and found a stapler on the desk. I snatched up the stapler and said, "If you hit me, I will fuck you up with this stapler!" My lack of fear paralyzed him and filled his heart with fear. The situation abruptly ended when other officers arrived on the scene to split us apart to prevent a potential fight.

There were no male lions in my pride to take down this large prey. There were no male lions in my pride to assist me. I quickly relied on my faith in Allah and tapped into my lioness spirit. What I thought was big prey was merely a hyena! With the protection of Allah and my success in conquering my fear, we prevailed. I had chosen not to bow to the created, but to the Creator!

Chapter 5
Fuck Or Fight

Cowardice is not acceptable in any lion pride! My mother, the original lioness, taught me that years ago. I remember running home from the park one day to inform her that my cousins were fighting a group of children. After running two blocks home and running up the stairs, my mom sensed something was wrong and met me at the door and opened it before I touched the handle.

"Richard and Bernice are fighting a group of kids at the park!" I reported. Tired, out of breath, and pumped full of fear like a chicken pumped full of steroids, I eagerly awaited her response.

"Let me get this straight," she said, "your cousins are fighting a group of kids, and you are standing here talking to me right now."

She angrily raised her voice to roar and shouted, "Get back over there and help your cousins fight. They could be dead right now!"

The roar in my mother's voice transferred the fear I was feeling in fighting the other children to fearing what she might do to me! I dashed back to the park and started swinging right and left hooks at anyone who was standing around. Unfortunately, the fight was over, and it turns out I was hitting innocent bystanders.

I was immediately met with gazing eyes from my cousins. "Why you run with your scary ass?" they asked.

I was saddened and disappointed in myself. I disappointed my favorite cousins. I let them down and sent a message to them that I could not be trusted and lacked loyalty. Oh yes, Mama, I got that lesson and learned it well!

I was a coward who let fear overtake me while they were the brave ones who stood strong in opposition and chose to fight. They tapped into the inner lion! They stood on truth, even when it got physical. They stood up to bullies while I ran. That was the last time I ran from a fight morally, verbally, or physically.

Step 3: Assessing the situation

My study of the lion species has shown me that a lion is not always at war and not always roaring in the jungle. The lion sits back and decides to hunt only when necessary. This same principle applies on a spiritual level. The lion within is dormant until awakened. Once the god in you is challenged by the devil in the environment, you have to make a decision. Is this the right time to be the lion? I do not disrespect my elders. Yes, a threat will awaken your inner lion(ness). However, in your assessment you must decide is it worth it to attack your elders. Our elders should be respected even when they are wrong.

Once you make that assessment, you must move to step four.

Step 4: Calling on Allah (God or the Creator) and releasing your inner lion

In the Holy Quran, there is no compulsion in Islam! Translation: life is about choices, and no one will force you to make the right or wrong choice. There is no time for mere belief today. It is time for you to "know" what is righteous and what is evil, what is truth and what is falsehood, what is God and what is devil. You must evolve into the "know" and leave belief for the *suckas*, the pretenders, the hypocrites! I say to those who say, "You have changed," "I have not changed; you have been allowed to see me for who I truly am. I am a 'Khalida,' doubled edged sword. I am both a warrior and a spiritual woman. I am a 'lioness!'"

When I first started working in a state prison, I was filled with straight fear. I don't know if it was because it was a male maximum facility, or if it was the smell of mustiness in the air, everywhere, I traveled in the prison. The smell was so strong it hit me when I first walked through the front door. For about a week, I constantly felt like I had to vomit and could not get that musty smell out of my nostrils or throat.

Fear is not a bad thing because it is fear that lets you know you are in a fight or flight situation. I was in the valley of decision. The inmates and officers smelled fear and had no problem letting me know. I had to think of a past experience where I was victorious and use it as motivation for this job.

I thought of my time as a young girl growing up on the west side of Chicago where I learned how to fight. I thought of all my years training in martial arts in Karate, Tae Kwon Do, and Jiu Jitsu. I thought of my years serving as an Honor Guard in the MGT and GCC Vanguard in the Nation of Islam. I immediately adjusted my thinking and chose to fight instead of flight. The lion had awakened!

My mother taught me to look people in the eyes when I talked to them because it demonstrated strength and self-respect. In the land of spiritual and physical human predators, it has a deeper meaning. When those sexual predators would stare at me, I could read their minds by reading their eyes. I could visualize all the dirty and physical things they wanted to do to me.

One of the first lessons I learned in the "joint" was "if you are a four in the world, then you are a seven or eight in the joint." What does this statement mean? It means that women who are less likely to be labeled attractive in the world will be labeled highly attractive in the prison environment. However, if you are a female officer that is considered "world pretty," you'd better look out! I was told by several inmates and officers that I was "world pretty."

Damn, that was definitely a lottery I did not want to win! It was the precursor to my experiences with both the male inmates and the male officers. My working environment was a microcosm of a world in which women are rated and given some numerical value based on superficial factors like body shape, leg length, hair length, polished nails, level of sexual openness to men, or, in my case, green eyes.

Poetic Combat

As a little girl, I always admired my mother's ability to verbally defeat others. I did not know that I had inherited this skillset until I became a grown woman. *Poetic Combat* was in our DNA.

My knowledge of *Poetic Combat* comes from the intelligence in the molecular structure of my DNA. Translation? It's in my DNA! My maternal DNA is Ethiopian, Tigray tribe to be exact.

The Tigray tribe of the Ethiopian people are known for many things. One, in particular, is the verbal skill known as P*oetic Comba*t. In Tigray folklore, an Ethiopian monk or saint, Tekle Haymanot, was credited for verbally outwitting the Devil with the usage of Poetic Combat. The Tigray people place a high value on their verbal skills and deem it important to be skillful and have clever ability to compose poetic couplets.

It's common in my family. We are quick-witted. My mom is a verbal master. She is not a very wordy person but will make quite an impact with one sentence. I remember her always saying "I'm a hard rock that can't be moved!" People would tremble when she said it because she said it with so much conviction and personality.

The teachings of the Most Honorable Elijah Muhammad encouraged mastery of the English language. In the teachings, it is imperative that you master the language that was used to enslave you. I, like Malcolm X, was liberated with the proper understanding and usage of words.

This tribal skillset served me well in the joint and gave me the verbal superiority that kept the predators in a state of confusion and defeat. My poetic combat skills had to be activated.

I recall Mother Tynetta helping me to activate *Poetic Combat* when she stressed the importance of the use of a dictionary while reading books or journals. She said it would deepen my word knowledge.

My belief in self was shattered when the school system scored me low in verbal and comprehension skills. However, Mother Tynetta Muhammad showed me that the enemy did not have the wisdom to assess me as an original Black Woman, a co-creator of God. She lit a fire under me!

I took a dictionary everywhere with me, looking up words I did not know the definition of to increase my understanding of the text. It was like a bomb going off in my soul, and that studying was a prelude to the Queen of Poetic Combat I would soon become!

War is psychic before it is physical. I won battle after battle, verbally and/or psychologically. As taught by The Most Honorable Elijah Muhammad, you hurl truth at falsehood until you knock out its brains!

Now, what you are about to hear will shock you! Throw out your thinking that women must be soft-spoken, feminine, dainty, and respectful. Those characteristics will make you a target in the belly of the beast (prison). A soft, dainty woman will be destroyed in this type of environment. In a male dominated, testosterone driven environment, the presence of the X chromosome is prey.

The presence of the X chromosome is not just a woman, but any man who is weak and fearful. I came in acting like prey; weak and fearful. However, I adapted. How did I adapt? I adapted by no longer fearing interactions with murderers, drug dealers, thieves, rapists, and sexual predators. There is a military philosophy that states that in order to defeat a predator, you have to turn them into prey. I quickly adapted to this philosophy and transformed into a predator.

Have you ever had a stare down with a sexual predator? I have! It is the most demoralizing experience for a woman. It will awaken every psychic gift that is buried deep into your DNA.

While being stared down by a sexual predator, you develop the four *clairs*: clairvoyance, clairaudience, clairsentience, and claircognizance. The four clairs are psychic abilities beyond the normal five senses. You experience seeing what he wants to do to you, hearing his thoughts on what he wants to do to you, and feel deep in your womb what he wants to do to you. You feel that a threat is evident, and you know that if he had an opportunity, you would be his victim. Victim, I am not! I refused to bow to the created; they bow to me!

I remember assisting other male officers with movement. Movement is escorting up to fifty inmates to another part of the prison for school, medical appointments, food, and yard. All of a sudden, the hairs on the back of my neck stood up, my stomach felt nauseous, my body temperature started rising, and my heart started pounding. I could feel someone's eyes on me. I looked to my left and found a sexual predator staring me down.

I called on Allah and tapped into my inner lioness. I had to use the innate weapon that Allah gives every woman. My tongue. The tongue is Woman's defaulted weapon to defeat a man who is physically stronger and is misusing his power. He is supposed to protect us, not prey on us.

Allah knew exactly what He was doing. How does a woman protect herself against a man who is in opposition to God and is acting like a devil? You bless her with the power of the tongue. Yes, our tongue can build a man up, and it can tear him down. I used it to protect myself, to tear a wicked man down. I coined a new phrase.

I stared right back into his eyes, aggressively walked toward him, and shouted, "Are we gonna Fuck or Fight? I love to do both. Either way it goes, I'm going to be on top!"

Those words reigned supreme! It was like I took a pin and poked a balloon to let out all of its air. His confidence and cockiness went limp like a wet noodle. All the other inmates and officers looked on in utter shock. The power he had suddenly left him and went into me. It was in that moment that I realized that I had tapped into the feminine power of God for a second time. The first was while giving birth, and now this. The delegation of God's power can make one feel pretty special. It set the rules of engagement for me moving forward in dealing with the male devil in the prison system.

I recall Minister Farrakhan stating that when a man controls the mind of a woman, her body will follow. Every day, men competed to control my mind like the many women who came before me. I chose to fight. I chose not to be the woman in some man's fantasy. In the book, *Force and Power of Being*, Minister Ava Muhammad states that you must have a stratagem to overpower the mind of your enemy. You must destroy the mind of your enemy in war and cause them to think like you!

I refuse to be trapped in a man's fantasy. Here is one example I have heard many times over the years: *I will fuck the shit out of you*. What woman wants to hear that through her entire work shift? Every woman becomes psychic after a while. We could hear their nasty thoughts by looking into their eyes. Officer training teaches you to ignore that type of behavior, but as a spiritual woman, a woman of God, I could not and would not allow any man to undress me and/or rape me with his eyes.

I say to my younger sisters who are consistently preyed upon by these types of men to apply this method and watch how the tables turn in your favor. My daughter came home one day and told me about how older men are always staring at her and her friends. I told her when they stare you down, do not turn away and do not blink. She tried it the very next time a man stared at her and it worked! The man turned away when he saw fearlessness and strength in her eyes.

Alpha Male vs. Beta Male

In the teachings of the Most Honorable Elijah Muhammad, we are taught the nature of the man and the woman. However, I was not prepared for the alpha/beta male dynamics I witnessed while working as an officer in a male prison facility. Whether women are present or not, the X Chromosome is always present.

What is the difference between an alpha and a beta male? Webster dictionary defines an "alpha male" as a dominant male, while Cambridge dictionary defines a "beta male" as a man who is not as successful or powerful as other men. In my experience, the alpha male is the man whom other men and women respect and honor. He is also magnetic and displays a quiet strength. He does not argue or compete with women. He is similar to the lion.

I have grown to hate the beta male because of his demoralizing behavior in the male-dominated or public environment. Why? The beta male is the man who wants to argue with women. He wants to go back and forth with a woman in front of everyone. He wants to steal the attention from the woman. He is the one who uses a woman to get the attention of other men.

You may ask why he would use a woman as a tool. Again, for the attention and respect of other men. He needs to beat you down physically, emotionally or spiritually to feel as successful and powerful as other men. I fought with beta males for seven years. Many, I worked side by side with, and many, I was responsible for keeping locked up.

A lieutenant pleaded with me not to call these male inmates "bitches," and out of respect for him and his concern for my safety, I agreed not to do it anymore. However, I never agreed to stop calling out the "bitch" in them, so I reworded the phrase and dropped it in a more intellectual way: "I need you to go find your Y Chromosome!"

I would not be used to solidify or prove some beta male's manhood to a group of alpha males. I was treated like a woman with no brain, no heart, and definitely no soul. I was treated like one big vagina that is present just to be a physical or mental repository for some pervert.

Female officer on deck!

There is a different type of fight when you are a woman fighting amongst and against men. You fight with the knowledge that if your fellow male officers are defeated, you are alone with no one to protect you. You are food for the wolves. I fought to control my fate. I refused to be din-din for the wolves. I fought to protect the purity and holiness of my womb.

Once I solidified my self-worth, the alpha males emerged to protect and honor me. I am grateful for my alpha male coworkers who protected me. I humbly thank the following officers with the following initials: DB, MT, MV, JB, DA, AC, KB, and many others.

I also want to give thanks to the incarcerated alpha males who shut down all disrespect of me. May Allah be pleased with you! I am forever grateful. I say to you that when we, as women, understand our worth and value and live the life of a virtuous woman, it activates something very special in a man. It activates the part of his nature that wants to honor, nurture, and protect us. I know. I lived it!

We Fight with Those who Fight with Us

Remember in chapter 2, I spoke of my Uncle Joey and how he introduced me to martial arts? Uncle Joey set the foundation for my relationship with Grand Master Abdul Aziz Muhammad, formally known as Grand Master Anthony Muhammad. He's not just my Grand Master, but my big brother. My brother from another mother. Grand Master is very passionate about teaching and produces the finest of students. He teaches his students both physically and spiritually. They are not just his students; they are forever family to him and his wonderful wife, my big sister Aziza.

He taught me how to use the art of Jiu Jitsu and how to effectively practice, master, and use it to defend myself against any enemy, male or female. It was in his class where I learned the knowledge and acquired the strength it takes to defend myself mentally and physically in a street fight or battle situation.

I remember in 1995, he moved to Chicago from Brooklyn, NY and opened his school. I was one of his first students in Chicago. In most martial arts schools, you are given a white belt when you enroll. However, in Grand Master's class, you had to *earn* your white belt. I earned my place in that class, as I earned a six-foot, first-place trophy in sparring, a fighting competition where whomever scores the most points striking their opponent wins. All of Grand Master's students left with trophies and also left quite the impression on the Windy City. The experience of fighting in tournaments with my martial arts class prepared me to fight with my fellow officers in the prison.

I remember running the yard one day with my coworker, a caring and wonderful brother who displayed mad love for his fellow officers. We were both acting sergeants that day. While he, I, and three other officers brought about fifteen to twenty inmates from yard, an inmate attacked him!

I was in shock and could not move! I froze for about three seconds and then love took over. My love for self, took control. My love for my battle buddy unfroze me. He was not going to fight alone, so I jumped into the fight! Crazy, right? I had to because I knew he would do the same for me, as he did for so many others. He was that type of dude! Whenever a fight begins, the person you are with is now your battle buddy and you are bonded for life. I am bonded with him and every officer who was present for life.

After the inmate struck him, the fight began, and I fearlessly kicked the inmate in his rib section. He quickly felt the kick and looked at me and kept fighting my battle buddy. I was disappointed in myself because it felt like I barely kicked him, so I kicked him again.

The first gallery (in prison each floor is called a gallery) became a stage. Inmates in their cells cheered and yelled like attendees in a Roman auditorium. I could hear them banging and kicking on their steel doors. It was loud like an afternoon in a coliseum. They wanted to see blood! They wanted to see a war!

We danced around the gallery like dancers performing a routine in a Beyonce video. I remember my battle buddy acting out a heavyweight bout. He was sticking and moving. I threw a punch and it landed on the side of the inmate's head. I then kneed him in the head.

All of a sudden, the cavalry came to our aid. My fellow coworkers who responded to the distress call engulfed us. About five officers moved in that unit like a dust storm. I was covered by several officers, and the fighting stopped once the officers regained control of the unit by locking up the free inmates from yard and taking down the one inmate who was the aggressor. The symbolism of those officers covering me by coming to my aid represented Allah's covering of me on that job. When you stand for truth, Allah is always present. He is always protecting me!

Later, I found out my kicks were harder than I thought. My husband, who worked at another prison at the time, came home and told me that the inmate who started the fight was transferred to his prison. The inmate saw his last name on his uniform and asked if he was kin to me. When my husband said yes, the inmate pulled up his shirt, showed him a bandaged rib, and said, "Look what she did to me!"

Wow! Allah was present on the scene. We were victorious because we were standing on truth!

Many of my dojo classmates went on to acquire black belts. I chose to complete my journey of education and vowed to come back to acquire my black belt at a later date.

Our life experience serves a purpose in our lives. We may not understand its purpose while we are experiencing it, but later in life we grow to accept and understand its value. It wasn't until I worked in corrections that I grew to really value Grand Master and the art form he taught me.

Step 5: Retreat and Seek Refuge in Allah (God)

The Holy Quran teaches us to stop fighting our enemy when they stop fighting us. I applied this principle to know when to stop the battle.

You cannot be in "lion mode" 24 hours a day. It's just too much! One must have balance. Exercising compassion and restraint at the right time can bring you Allah's mercy and protection. It demonstrates that you are one who operates on righteous principles and fairness. Administration of Allah's laws must be fair and just.

Let me share one of my past experiences where properly exercising Step 5 saved me from destruction while in a position of authority. While working as a correctional officer on the midnight shift, I worked in a unit where three officers were assigned to secure four separate wings. Each wing had approximately sixty-eight male inmates. I was the officer assigned to a central location to observe all inmates and officers by camera. One officer was on a wing, the second officer was on a different wing, while I observed the security cameras.

My view of one officer was obstructed, and the other officer was on a separate wing dealing with an inmate with chest pains. I was in quite the dilemma. The officer dealing with the inmate with chest pains had to leave the unit, and I had to do something about the officer on the wing that I could not see because he was surrounded by inmates. While yelling at the inmates through a thick glass to move away from the officer, an inmate on another wing banged on the wing's door to inform me that he also had chest pains. I stopped yelling at the inmates on the first wing and redirected my aggression to the other inmate with the chest pains.

Minutes later, medics arrived to assist the inmate. He was taken to health care and returned about three to four hours later. The next day, I went on the wing and requested the inmate come out to the main floor of the dorm-like wing. He came out to the main floor, and I instructed all the inmates to listen up.

According to the teachings of the Most Honorable Elijah Muhammad, when you make your error in the public, you are corrected in the public. I stated to him and the group of inmates that I disrespected him as a man by yelling at him in front of other men in that manner and asked for his and the others' forgiveness. He humbly accepted, and our interactions from that point were honorable. I also gained a high level of respect from the other male inmates; they already knew I was an officer who did my job regardless of what other inmates thought, but now they understood that I was true to my religious principles.

In case you didn't know, inmates have a memory like an elephant; they never forget. They will kick your ass over something that happened five years ago. They never forget! About a year later, I worked day shift in the worst cell house in the prison. I was assigned two gallery (2nd floor) and was informed by my sergeant that I had a new inmate moving on my gallery. I walked the inmate up the stairs while he carried his mattress to his cell.

As I walked him to his cell, I thought to myself that he looked very familiar. Once he put the mattress on the gallery, I contacted the tower to open his cell. While waiting, I asked him where was he housed before? He reminded me of the location and I immediately remembered him and his situation. It took only about one minute for the tower officer to open the cell, but that one minute seemed like forever. In that one minute, I thanked Allah for His guidance, His mercy and His protection.

It was a moment of epiphany. If I had not handled the previous situation appropriately, the inmate, who was approximately 6'3' and 180 lbs., could have given me a pumpkin head! In the prison system, an officer can get a beatdown in a minute or less, so he had more than enough time to complete the task. Now, you understand like I understand. If I would not have apologized to that inmate, the outcome could have been a lot different. All Praise Be to Allah, I submitted to His guidance and wisdom and my obedience resulted in His mercy and protection!

I could share hundreds of stories of triumph in corrections with you, but we would be here all day. However, I will share one more story, one that gave me inner peace and let me know that I passed the test and graduated into a lioness, and battle had become a part of my nature. I no longer felt fear when it was time for battle. I felt an overwhelming sense of peace when the very inmates who waged war on me respected my battle experience and feared me, instead of me fearing them.

I knew my mission was over, and it was time for me to move on. My intuition revealed to me that my time in the uniform as an officer was coming to an end. It was time to start a new chapter in my life. My peers wondered how I could work around inmates and not feel fear. Easy! I was a *clicker*.

I remember working with several other officers to escort almost fifty inmates to a housing unit. There were two officers in the front, two to five officers in the back, and another officer and me in the middle walking alongside the inmate line. I always walked along the line when I needed to be the enforcer. Me being the enforcer depended on the number of alpha males who worked with me. In the presence of alpha males, I fell totally back and let them be the lions they were created to be. However, that day was different. I wasn't with a crew of alpha males.

The inmates were instructed not to talk while paired up in two lines. All they could hear was *click, click, click*. My fellow officers were unbothered by the clicking sound because they knew it oh, so well. Once we reached the destination, we stopped the line. However, in the silence everyone could hear *click, click, click*.

In my peripheral vision, I caught one inmate staring at me and I stared right back, looking deeply into his eyes without blinking. The battle was on. The first to look away would lose, the one with the strongest will would win. He broke his stare and gazed downward at my hands to notice the ink pin I held. He immediately looked back into my eyes and I smiled at him. Why? I smiled not out of victory, but because I knew that he knew that if he flinched in my direction, the ink pen would be lodged into his jugular vein.

As my fellow officer addressed the men, I heard one inmate whisper to another, "What's that clicking noise?"

"That's Officer Muhammad," the other inmate said. "She clicks her pen all the time. She crazy, man. Don't mess with her. She'll stab you with her pen!"

Yes, the pen is mightier than the sword! My Badge# was 12565 and the numbers in my badge added up to the number 19. The most honorable Elijah Muhammad teaches us that the number 19 represents the signature of Allah. Allah shielded me for seven years from danger as he fashioned me into the lioness I am today. Once I dropped the badge, I emerged from the shadows like a phoenix rising from its own ashes. I'm honored to have been protected by Allah and His angels. I vow to pay it forward by passing on Allah's wisdom that I used for my protection, so that you may be enlightened and protected.

Walking in my own atmosphere

I am one who walks in my own atmosphere. The early years of my life started out on the west side of Chicago. At approximately 5 years old, my mother and I moved to the western suburbs of Chicago, but she sent me back to the west side on weekends. She also sent me to different military bases to spend the summer with family members who were stationed in places like Altus Air Force

Base, OK, Fort Sill, OK, Scott Air Force Base, IL, and other states like Texas, Georgia, Missouri, and California.

There were many principles such as self-discipline, service, respect for authority, and honor in the military environment that helped shape me into the woman I am today. These principles were ingredients to form my eternal soldier, and they have guided me in my decision-making throughout my adulthood.

Self-discipline is one of the most obvious. When people meet me, they see that I am very disciplined and can easily be disturbed by undisciplined people who display a lack of control of their emotions and actions.

The second principle is service. One joins the military to be of service to their country. I believe that service is important and necessary in order for your community to flourish. You can grab any book on leadership in any bookstore, and service is identified as a required attribute for great leaders in the business sector, athletic world, and on the battlefield.

Respect for authority is another important principle that I learned and learned well. I remember my militant upbringing. Military families can be very strict on their children. The lesson of "children are to be seen and not heard" resonates deep with me as it solidifies the fact that children and adults are not on the same level. I learned to never talk back and to obey the orders of the adults in my family. In my family adults represent authority and if you respect the authority in your household you would respect authority figures in society. It was just that simple. To this day, I respect my elders because they represent authority and leadership.

Honor is a principle that great men and women display. I was taught to never behave in public in a way that would embarrass or shame my family. I have grown to be a person of great honor and will not behave in any way that will bring dishonor to myself or my family.

Along with childhood and military principles, I learned additional principles by observing Big Donna. I got from her what I could not get from my big sister Rhonda, may Allah be pleased with her soul. Big Donna taught me in words and in actions. She was unbothered by all the guys who cat called her and hounded her for her phone number. She kept her focus on me. She basically ignored them. She was classy and didn't feed off of men's attention when she was with me.

She taught me how to dress because she wore the most stylish clothing. I never once saw her wear anything that would cause men to lose their respect for her. I watched how she carried herself among men, and I learned that a decent woman is unbothered by men, and she must be guarded and not easy to get. Self-value was her banner. I thank her and deeply love Big Donna!

Because of what I learned from Big Donna, I do not submit to sexism, racism, or capitalism. Submitting to the "isms" is submitting to the enemy, to the Devil. Any man who wants to sexualize me is my enemy. I do not attract those types of men; my energy vibrates too high for them. I just vibrate them right out of my atmosphere. I approach life like I'm Mary, the mother of Jesus. I reject all men unless they come to me as God in the form of a well-made man. I'm producing a Jesus on a higher level! Take that approach and watch them vibrate their weak asses out of your atmosphere!

Choosing to tap into the lion(ness) within you is a spiritual decision. It is the road less traveled. I made the conscious decision to do so; it is the path of no return. In order to become more aggressive, I put red meat back in my diet. I needed the ability to go from zero to 100 in seconds, and red meat gave me the ability.

You will leave many loved ones behind because you will be elevating yourself to a higher level in which so few reside. Greatness is not achieved by the masses. I challenge you to elevate yourself to a higher level. The very reason why you continue to suffer is because you choose to remain on a lower level. Elevate and watch how quickly you minimize your suffering.

As women, we have become numb in this society to sexual misconduct from men and even some women. It is so bad that I had a female co-worker touch me on my backside and ask, "What are you doing, your backside looks different."

I laughed it off and said, "Squats, girl, squats!" I laughed to hide the fact that I was so uncomfortable with her actions. Sadly, several people in the room laughed, most of the were women. We have accepted this abuse from men and now we are doing it to ourselves!

It is possible you may not agree with my point of reference as to why it is necessary for a woman to have a lioness spirit. You may ask why should a woman be a lioness? I will tell you why. We are living in a time where men are preying on women through domestic violence, sex trafficking, and rape. According to www.unwomen.org, 35% of women have experienced physical and/or sexual intimate partner violence, or sexual violence by a non-partner; approximately 137 women are killed by a member of their family every day and less than 40 % of the women who experience violence seek help of any sort.

A lion(ness) takes what he(she) wants and claims it for him or herself. We must re-claim our chastity and dignity. Are you with me? Or are you ok with being a sexual object? It's your decision. Are you going to FUCK or FIGHT?

Chapter 6
Healing From Battle

After a lion or lioness returns home from a battle, it is obligatory to go into a state of healing, meditation, and prayer. Why? Physical, emotional, or spiritual battles result in wounds.

Today, women living in a paternalistic society experience wounds physically, emotional and spiritually. A paternalistic society is one where the value of Woman is rejected, and her worth holds no value. It is a society where the role of women is reduced to being sexual tools of entertainment, baby-making machines, and punching bags for men. It is important for Woman to restore what has been lost.

The spirit is amazingly intelligent. It will alert you that something is wrong. It will inform you that the spiritual or physical programming of the body has been altered. My soul communicated this message to me for some time. My body and spirit were demonstrating illness. I started praying and asking Allah for guidance. Allah provided me with the knowledge I sought and revealed to me that I suffer from the *Jesus Syndrome,* desire to sacrifice myself to save others.

Prayer is asking God for the answer, and meditation is listening quietly to receive the answer. During one of my meditation sessions, while meditating with sodalite, a crystal that helps you see and accept your inner truth, I was able to receive the message that I sacrifice my well-being for the benefit of others, even when it is not warranted or appreciated.

When I was twelve years old, I was in the line to jump off the diving board into nine feet of water. A scrawny little boy in front of me convinced the lifeguard he was big enough to dive in without drowning. The lifeguard told him to demonstrate his swimming ability by swimming across the pool. He successfully completed the task and was allowed to jump off the diving board. However, after jumping off the diving board into nine feet of water, although a swimmer, he panicked and started going under. I looked at the lifeguard, but he was occupied with a beautiful girl in a swimsuit, more aware of the girl in front of him than the young boy drowning in the pool. I counted the number of times the boy went under as I stood at the top of the diving board.

The voice from within told me to jump in and save him as he went under for the third time. I eagerly jumped in, which was a big mistake. The little boy latched onto me, and I could not control him. He kicked and swung like a mad man, taking me down with him. We both went under twice as I fought to save us both. All of a sudden, the lifeguard jumped in and saved us.

"Why did you do that?" he yelled. "You could have caused both of you to drown!"

I was so hurt and ashamed. I was made to feel like I was the cause of this traumatic experience. I was only trying to save the little boy, and I was treated as if I was drowning him. All of my peers at the pool asked me why did I do that, but no one saw what I saw. I saw a drowning boy and a lifeguard who was distracted by a female, and a pool full of people who were so into their own fun that they failed to notice the drowning boy.

I ran home and told my mom the story. She hugged me and assured me that I did the right thing, but her love and support came with a warning: "You can't save everybody!"

This was a lesson I did not learn that summer because the little boy almost drowned again in nine feet of water, and I jumped in to save him again. The results were the same and I did not regret it. I still have not learned that lesson. I continue to try to save those who do not want to be saved, can't be saved, or must be saved by someone else. The only lesson I have learned from this history is that I suffer from the "Jesus Syndrome." My experiences of sacrificing myself to save others created the need for me to heal. I needed to heal spiritually and desperately seeking a healing outlet.

In March of 2019, I attended the "Then the Sun Rose" women's retreat. I participated in a couple of workshops led by a sister named Khetnu Nefer. In her Egyptian Yoga session, she taught me the power of speaking to the womb. I thought to myself, "I am not going to do that. This woman is crazy!"

However, after that session I learned that the womb is where the woman's emotions dwell. Many of our woman issues are affected by emotions that have developed by bad relationships, traumatic experiences, and self-hatred.

Khetnu instructed all of us to lay on our backs. I was nervous and skeptical at the same time, experiencing feelings of hope and doubt at the same time. How is that possible? I clearly don't know, but I felt them at the same damn time! Once we were on our backs, she guided us through breathing exercises.

"Breathe in slowly. Now exhale," she said repeatedly. As I followed her instructions, my body became still, and I could feel myself gain control over my body. I felt confident, like a pilot in the cockpit. I was in control.

Once we completed the breathing exercises, we were instructed to speak to our womb. I was nervous and uncertain, not sure if this exercise would work, or worse, the exercise would work for everyone else but me! I felt like a young girl speaking to a boy for the very first time. I spoke to my womb for the first time ever. As Khetnu facilitated this exercise, I asked my womb questions and guess what happened? It started talking back!

I know! I know! You think I am crazy, too. Hell, I thought I was going crazy, laying on the floor having a conversation with my womb. I could see myself trying to explain this to my husband and my mother, my two confidantes. As I described the activity, I could visualize them picking up their phone to call the funny farm.

My womb was tense and anxious at the beginning of this exercise, but at the end, my womb felt more liberated. My womb felt like I felt when I spoke my mind freely. I was now a believer. I had a toxic womb. I was a different woman after the exercise, and I was hungry for more self-discovery, more expression of self-love and healing.

Khetnu also conducted my vaginal steam. I signed up for all the spa services because I knew in my heart that I was in need of healing. The vaginal steam was very intimate. In this session, she explained how she formulated the herbs based on my questionnaire answers. My occupation, work environment, age, sexual activity, and child-bearing history were all taken into consideration.

At the beginning of the session, my body temperature felt like it was 60 degrees, orchestrated by fear and anger. We began the steam, and the herbs made me relaxed. I felt like a patient in a hospital who had just been administered medication, and it was working. The tightness in my womb left as she broke down how my womb was negatively affected by my toxic work environment.

Her knowledge of womb care and her openness to share her personal battles with health and how it led her to assist women in their own healing warmed my body like an electric blanket. As she spoke, her loving words and energy covered my body and heated me to a comfortable temperature of approximately 73 degrees.

After my vaginal steam session, I felt like a new woman. The burden I was carrying was released and I felt lighter physically. Most of all, I felt a cloud of love over me, and it felt good. *Please contact Khetnu Nefer, CEO of A Soulful Touch Wellness, LLC at <u>www.asoulfultouch.net</u>.*

Unlike many other women, my vaginal steam helped heal me. In her book, *A New Unit of Measurement*, Minister Ava Muhammad states that women have a physical and spiritual womb. My physical womb had been healed, and it activated the power of my spiritual womb to teach the Word of God. I knew I had a testimony to share. I knew what the women in my lineage did not know. I was able to complete a process of healing that many women deserve and need to experience.

I returned home with a new mission to use my platform to help my sisters activate the self-healing gene within self. As excited as I was to realize this, I thought about my grandmother and how I wished I could have passed this learning on to her. I learned this lesson after her death!

Momma

This section was inspired by my grandmother, Velma Jo Booker. Many would agree that she was an angel. My grandmother loved the Lord and thought it was necessary to demonstrate her love for Him by loving and caring for others.

Velma Jo Booker raised me in my early years. My mother gave birth to me prematurely, requiring me to spend several months in a hospital incubator. This time spent in an incubator robbed me of nurturing. My mom had just lost my sister, Rhonda, and she was in a state of depression. She had just lost her first born to Sickle Cell Anemia and was on the verge of losing another child.

The doctors were unsure if I would live or die due to my special entrance into this world. I came three months too soon, due to a slip on a wet bathroom floor. My mother had been washing clothes on a washboard when she heard the phone ring. She quickly rose from her knees to answer it, but she fell and broke her water bag. Hence, I was born. I was literally called into existence!

After coming home from the hospital, my mother sat in a chair and stared out of the window. She was emotionally gone. She was temporarily checked out. She was grieving. My Aunt Emma called my grandma and said, "come get this baby!"

My grandma came and got me, raised me, nurtured me, and gave my mother time to heal. My early years with her were like that of a seed planted in good productive soil. I was being watered daily by my grandmother. All that was raised by her was raised in good soil, as she raised so many children whom she did not bore, including my mother. Her knowledge, wisdom and love gave me life like water and sun gives a plant life.

She taught me God first, and how to love others second. She taught me how to cook, clean, and take care of family. She taught me religion and psychology, as she taught from the Holy Bible and the Diagnostic and Statistical Manual of Disorders. She had aspirations to be a Doctor of Clinical Psychology but did not pursue them in order to remain a devoted wife and mother. However, I witnessed her help several of her friends pursue their PhDs.

She loved children with special needs and wanted to be their clinical doctor. I remember her accurately diagnosing houseguests. These people were narcissistic, schizophrenic, depressed and out of their damn minds, but "Momma," as she was affectionately called by everyone in the neighborhood, loved them all the same.

Momma taught me how to open my heart and love everyone. She said, "family ain't about blood," as she assured me that her love and acceptance was sincere. She taught me that family extended beyond blood. It was about the family that God brings together through love and circumstance.

She fed the neighborhood delicious meals, cakes, and pies. Most of all, she fed them love, and her funeral procession proved that to be true! I used to get angry with her for loving everyone because I knew they would use her up. And they did. However, as I grew older, I found that I am becoming Momma because my heart is big and open like hers was.

The only thing she failed to teach me was how to take care of self because she died not learning that lesson. She cared for others until it killed her. She sacrificed herself on a cross like Jesus, literally dying for the sins of others. She sacrificed her life raising other people's children along with her own. If you made errors, she was there to give you God's word, she was there to give you forgiveness and acceptance, she was there to give you money and be a light at the end of the tunnel. Her love for others superseded her love for self.

Guess what, Momma! I got that doctorate you always wanted, and I learned what you could not teach me, self-care! How to heal myself! Let me teach you, Momma! Let me teach you, Black Woman, how to heal the generational curse of passing down unhealed pain. Let me teach you, Momma!

As I meditate with Moldavite (crystal for accessing spiritual realms) and Smokey Quartz (crystal for remaining grounded while meditating), I have come into the realization that the frequency I operate on is one of love. I operate on the love frequency that was passed down to me from Momma. I am on 432 Hz (healing frequency), where Allah has instructed me to be.

What frequency are you operating on? Self-hatred? High Sexuality? Moving like a Boss? Career Lady? It is obvious you are on a lower frequency because you are reading this book! Get off of 440 Hz (standard radio frequency for music) and elevate your thinking!

Allah speaks to us through messages. He delivered a message to me multiple times until I received it. Two years ago, I rode past AbbVie company every week. After about a month of seeing this company, I felt that God was sending a spiritual message or instruction to me.

One day, I went home and looked up the company on the Internet and learned that it was a pharmaceutical company. I did not understand what that had to do with me until two years later when I saw the a commercial for AbbVie Company. The commercial communicated the duties and mission of the company. I learned that it was innovative in the field of medicine and was dedicated to healing the sick. I experienced an epiphany. Allah finally blessed me with the meaning of this message. He was informing me of the mighty work he was preparing for me to do. He was preparing me to be a portal, a conduit that He uses to heal the very people who have heard and accepted His message of truth.

He is now using me to deliver a message of truth that will heal people of the spiritual illness that has consumed their souls and contributed to their physical and spiritual sickness. My message is researched and is as innovative on the spiritual level as the AbbVie Company has become on a physical level. Allah has blessed me to deliver the truth from Him in a modern way that is needed for this era. It is one that is needed to destroy the modern devil so the righteous can again reign supreme.

Chapter 7

The Five Steps To Awakening The Lion (Ness) Spirit Within In Review

Let's review the five steps in Awakening the Lion(ness) Spirit Within: (1) Learning the Knowledge of the Devil, (2) Learning the Knowledge of God, (3) Assessing the Situation, (4) Calling on Allah (God) and Releasing Your Inner Lion, and (5) Retreat and Seek Refuge in Allah. These five steps will require great concentration and self-discipline. Don't let that frighten or discourage you from trying to achieve a high level of greatness. It is not a task; it is more of a process.

A process must be applied step by step in order to be successful. However, mastery is not expected overnight and will not be obtained until exercised consistently. It is imperative that you do not discount the importance of searching for, identifying, learning about, and conquering the devil within.

True spirituality and God-like qualities will not be obtained until the enemy of God is dealt with and conquered. I quote my mother in saying, "The Devil is a lie!"

The devil within will lie to you and convince you that it is your friend and protector. The devil will deceive you into thinking that God does not exist; nor does He exist within. Be not be deceived. The Devil will manifest itself in the form of your ego, coming to protect you, to teach you, and to love you. Wrong! The Devil comes to make you vulnerable to demoralizing self-attacks and attacks by others. The Devil comes to convince you that you are better than others and justifies of mistreatment of others. The Devil comes to trick you into thinking you are the constant victim.

It is your responsibility to hang out or parlay in the depths of your mind, heart, and soul. Search for the devil spirit that lurks in the darkness. Face it. Go to war with the darkness of self. Go to war with the Devil. Do not come out until you are the victorious one. Do not come out until you have learned that you can be Devil or you can be God. It is a choice. Don't come out until you have acquired the crown.

Come out knowing that Devil and God are two contrasting states of mind. Be confident that you fought the devil within until you experienced the "aha" moment, the moment where you realized that you control your own fate. You control what you think, what you accept, and how you choose to behave in this world. Take the knowledge of the Devil to defeat him and grow into the knowledge of God.

Now that you have become God in human form, you recognize God in every creation, in every word, and in every form. You recognize His voice when you hear it. You identify with His message of truth when it is spoken. Most of all, you will know when it comes out of your mouth. Why will you know it? You will know it because it will become a part of who you are.

You can now assess the presence of God or the Devil. You now have the wisdom to determine what is from God and what is not. The true and living God has blessed you with his coloring, and now you see truth and can easily separate it from falsehood. You are truth. You can only see, speak or do truth. You have become the lion in scripture. You will now go forth in the land and speak the truth that comes from written books, from God-inspired scripture, and what is extracted from the womb of the universe.

The question is what happens if when you make the assessment that what you are seeing or experiencing is not of God? No one will have to tell you because you will just know. I didn't need anyone to tell me to jump into the pool to save the little boy; I just knew. The Devil in this situation was the lifeguard's weakness for women that distracted him from doing his job, which was to save those who would be in danger of losing their lives by drowning.

No one had to tell me that the sexual predator I encountered in the prison system who had filthy thoughts of sexually assaulting me was wrong and criminal; I just knew. The God within just knew what to do in the situation because I called on Allah (God), and so will you! You will call on Allah (God) and release the inner lion. You will hurl truth at falsehood until you knock out its brains. Falsehood has intellect. However, truth or knowledge of God has *supreme* intellect!

You will call on Allah (God) and let Him guide you. You will defeat falsehood. You will defeat the external devil because you already defeated the internal devil. The hardest part has already been accomplished. Step 1, Learning the Devil, is the hardest step. You are no longer the weak or the weak-hearted one. You are the strongest one!

Now retreat and return back to Allah (God). Return the power that you borrowed back to the owner. The power we carry as little gods comes from the original source, the big God. Understanding this notion is very important because it will keep you spiritually healthy by healing your spirit that was damaged by going to war with falsehood, the devil in the land, and it will keep you from thinking you are greater than the true and living God.

Chapter 8
The Lioness As A Leader

I asked Allah to use me to help spiritually elevate Black women. He put me in the belly of the beast! A prison where sexism, racism, self-hatred, decadence, deceit, and manipulation are the norm. I maintained my loyalty to Him. In my eight years, I have never wavered from my Islam, from my Allah! I qualified myself to be an educator and a teacher to my people.

The teachings of the Most Honorable Elijah Muhammad instruct us to qualify ourselves for positions that are awaiting us. The masses of people are oppressed and suffering. A new type of leadership must stand up. One that is as bold and as brave as a lion. One that is not afraid to stand up to and for the people. One that is not afraid to stand up against the oppressive leadership that is now in place and must be dethroned.

You may think that you do not have what it takes to be a leader. However, I have shared five steps with you that I use to Awaken the Lion(ness) within. You must learn the knowledge of the Devil, learn the knowledge of God, assess the situation, call on Allah (God) and unleash the lion within, and retreat and seek refuge in Allah (God). Aligning yourself with the power of God will empower you to be the lion(ness) that our society needs in this era.

There was no manager, teacher, or politician to anoint the great leaders of God that you read about in your scriptures or read about in your history books. These great leaders saw what needed to be done and stood up. Once they stood up, God empowered them, He backed them. Now, you read about them!

This could be you! Who's stopping the sex trafficking in your neighborhood? It could be you. Who's stopping the gun violence in your neighborhood? It could be you. Who's stopping the police brutality in your neighborhood? It could be you!

I asked myself what I would do about the oppression of Black women in this society. I had to answer my own question. I started an organization and started teaching what I know. I co-founded Royal Empress with Akilah Shabazz. Royal Empress is an organization that is spiritually and mentally reawakening the original Black woman by providing educational training tools and resources designed to inspire, empower, and elevate one sister at a time.

We have a bi-weekly podcast, *Conversations with the Royal Empress*, with more than seventy topics that address various issues considering spiritually uplifting Black women. Our podcast is available on YouTube, Itunes, Google Play, and Podbean, and can be accessed any time, or followed on Facebook, Twitter, and Instagram.

We have also started the *Royal Empress Naomi Project*, a mentoring program for Black women ages eighteen and older. Our objective is to pair women who have successfully navigated through spiritual, emotional, financial, and career-oriented situations to mentor those who are trying to mimic their success. To learn more about our organization, *Conversations with Royal Empress*, and *Naomi Project*, go to www.royalempress.org.

In times of travail, a roving leader emerges. A roving leader is one who steps up to perform leadership duties in the absence of legitimate leadership. As you read the words of this book, legitimate leadership is being abased. They are being brought down by Allah (God). The leadership that forged the shaping of this country is dissolving right before our eyes. You don't have to be a minister, teacher, policeman, businessman, or politician to be a leader.

I have laid the blueprint out for you to follow. Use the Five Steps to Awaken the Warrior Spirit Within to become brave and fearless. You must be a lion and demonstrate real leadership among a pack of hyenas (weak leadership). What will you do? Will you tap into the lion(ness) within? I leave you as I greet you with As Salaam Alaikum, which means peace be unto you!

Words from those who know me!

Thank you for reading "Lion(ness): Awakening the Warrior Spirit Within. Now that you have read the book, you are aware of the five steps I performed in order to awaken my inner lioness. I pray that you effectively implement Learning the Knowledge of the Devil, Learning the Knowledge of Allah (God), Assessing the Situation, Calling on Allah (God) and Releasing Your Inner Lion, and Seeking Refuge in Allah (God) will help you tap into the lion(ness) within.

I asked my peers three questions. What did you think of me when you first met me? What have you learned from me? Where do you think my growth and development will take me in the future?

Here are their sincere responses: (listed below along with their initials)

"A Beautiful Sister" by ST

"That you were sincere and kind. You are someone that can see greatness in others" DT

"My clone. Here is a person laid back, enjoy being around others but don't like dumb stuff. As I worked side by side with you, I watched you develop this strong voice. I am so proud of you. I know there is nothing you can't do. I see you as a motivational speaker." LH

"Beautiful Queen." BH

"Warrior" LM

"Beautiful, cool, pleasant, nice, hardworking, high spirited, fearless, helpful, and determined." CM

"Beautiful" EB

"You are very beautiful inside and out." RI

"I asked you if you were wearing contacts? Lol. I see you as a blunt and honest person and as a leader." DD

"When we first met, your energy spoke to me first before you did. You are definitely an inspiration of what you do for our people when it comes to supporting others." CM

"Extra super out of my league, like I don't even want to really talk to you. Deep, extra smart. You are supper passionate in your belief and I appreciate your passion. You are not easily persuaded, strong, and confident. I envision you heading a powerful women's movement, standing against injustices for Black People everywhere. You are Malcolm, Martin, and Rosa and every other Black hero." DK

"Your eyes are captivating. Your level of wisdom and intellect is essential. You will educate others with truth and free them from societal bondage" CP

"This beautiful, intelligent, hardworking, go-getter, strong black woman. What I learned from you is that you are about business, and you don't start anything, but will finish it. You can and will do anything you set your mind to and have a special love for your people. You are very genuine. As you are growing, I see you reaching for the sky, which has no limit." QC

"I felt complete sisterhood the moment you first reached out to me. You taught me to be spiritually awakened in all settings. Socially and professionally. You will continue to serve as a servant of God, reaching women on a larger landscape. May God continue to speak through you." LM

"She is stunning. Behind a smile there is always an untold story. I believe you will be a teacher to women and for women. Women who are mentally traumatized. The capacity on how this will manifest is unclear, but Allah says is so it shall be." AA

"When I first met you, we were starting the academy. I was immediately at ease and comfortable around you. Talking to you calmed me more times than I can count and I'm so grateful that the universe brought us together and you were my bunk mate.

I have learned a lot from you. Strength, spirituality, crystal knowledge, patience, and self-love. I really have learned to own my spiritual side and not be afraid to be more vocal about it from you. When I think of you, I picture a strong female warrior! You are going to continue to grow and evolve and educate us all. I can't wait to see the amazing things you will do as you continue on your journey." EL

"Very strong-willed. Push the wrong button and you just might be sorry. You provided knowledge for my will and desire. Through you came the confirmation I sought after in certain areas of my life. To higher measures of life…you have equipped yourself spiritually and with knowledge and essential tools one needs. You have options. Continue to grow my sister. The sky awaits you." LC

"She sure is smart and beautiful." NT

"Down to Earth and well-spoken. Wasn't arrogant or trying to be the center of attention. I think whatever you choose in life you will do very well." RW

"Pleasant, stand up personality. Embraces the lioness within with confidence, risking all for what she believes in. Your growth will take you exactly where you want to go, and beyond." LP

"Beautiful strong black woman. A no-nonsense personality. Yet kind and loving." CB

"A beautiful quiet storm. Your eyes are very mysterious, however, revealing. I learned from you and being around you. That you are very educated but not just book smart if that makes sense. I learned that you are very trustworthy, painfully and respectfully honest. When I'm around you, we dig into each other without fear. I've understood peace being around you not that the storm may not be going on but that we get so caught up in higher learning that nothing else exists in that moment. I learned that you are a true sister and it makes me want to be better. I have to go back and read the other questions I'll be back. There are so many layers to you. You are multi-dimensional so skies the limit. You can't put a cap on greatness Queen." AH

"When I first met you all I thought was BIG SISTER going to have me fighting, everyday! I learned patience, self-worth, demand respect from my peers, and to love thyself from you. Your growth, I've witnessed is amazing.

Keep reaching for the stars because you definitely shining bright. Love you Sister." DB

"Well my perspective is different because you knew me before I knew you. However, I hold this memory of you sleeping on the lounge chair at Grandpa's house next to the piano and thinking to myself what I thought of you. I was between the ages of 4 and 7 years old. You were asleep, but your eyes were open, I thought you must be a special kind of human. I had never seen that, and at that age in my mind, it was like watching someone breathe under water.

It wasn't rude, I thought you were unbothered but passionate. Like, you didn't care about small things. You were always vocal about something rather it be your music, religion or diet choices. I thought you were smart, and I respected you. I used to observe and think, why are they challenging her? She will do what she wants and it's never a wrong thing. I liked you because you had an individual personality and was not like most people. I always liked your smile and your eyes. I imagined your life was like that of someone I watched on "A Different World" and I always wondered what you did outside of familiar surroundings.

You were always the most intriguing and I wanted to ask you a million questions, but you would run us kids away, so instead I'd just watch and listen. I also thought you could fight. I had a lot of questions when you got married the first time. I was like but why? Yeah these were thoughts between those ages during those nuptials." BN

A Special Thank You

First and foremost, I want to express my gratitude to those who made this book possible. I thank Dr. Elisa Bell for her guidance and wisdom with this project. Dr. Bell is my mentor, and my Naomi. I am grateful that she is in my life. This book would not have been possible without her.

I want to extend a big thank yo to my writing coach, author Tony Lindsey. He was so authentic and skillful in pulling my personal experiences out of me and showing me, the value and impact my words will have on my reading audience. Tony is unforgettable!

I must thank my wonderful sister, Akilah Shabazz. My sister from another mother, the one who came for me while I was fighting on the spiritual battlefield in the wilderness of North America. I thank her for showing me the importance of self-healing! I could not have healed myself without the great works of this sister!!!

Many people have friends, I have a tribe. I would not be the woman I am today if it was not for Yaa, Akilah, Andrea, Khetnu and Tanita. Your healing and nurturing love helped to activate the healer in myself. Your work with me is not over! I am deeply appreciative of who you all are as women and how you have touched me! Hooty Hoo!!!

I am grateful for having the opportunity to know and love Dr. Steffie Turner, may Allah be pleased with her. She shined light on my greatness and showed it to me. She saw me in a way no other person has ever seen me. I miss our long spiritual conversations. The conversations where we would crack atoms (discuss high level conversations). I miss you Steffie aka The Oracle!

I am blessed to be the woman I am today thanks to a wonderful man I call my king. Thank you, Sweetie, for helping to activate my inner lion. Your living example of living the word of God and your words of wisdom inspire me each and every day. I love you forever.

Mother is a powerful word, powerful expression and powerful act. Grateful to my mother for being an angelic example of righteousness, of wisdom and strength.

I'm so honored to be your child and have come from your womb. You are my universe!!!

CPSIA information can be obtained
at www.ICGtesting.com
Printed in the USA
LVHW111802291021
701929LV00013B/1627